Why Life Sucks

and what you can do about it

Todd Hayen, PhD

TABLE OF CONTENTS

WHY LIFE SUCKS

...the main trouble with human beings is their tendency to become engaged in the 'triviality of everyday-ness' (to borrow Heidegger's phrase), in the suffocating world of their personal preoccupations. And every time they do this, they forget the immense world of broader significance that stretches around them. And since man needs a sense of meaning to release his hidden energies, this forgetfulness pushes him deeper into depression and boredom, the sense that nothing is worth the effort.

~Colin Wilson

Actually, life doesn't suck. Life just *is*. Sometimes, though, it certainly feels like it sucks. I titled this booklet *Why Life Sucks* because I wanted to get your attention. If you are looking for help most likely you are going through some difficult times, and although you may not have come to the final conclusion that life sucks, you probably are wondering why things are so difficult.

The first thing I will say to you is this: You are not alone. Many people fall into the deep pit of loneliness, and the despair that goes with it, wondering why everyone else seems to be able to handle their tough times reasonably well—but it seems impossible for them to get a foothold. In fact, I would venture to say that everyone at least one time in their life, and more than likely many times, feels the way you do right now. Some feel worse. Some can eventually get out of it. Some cannot. But most of them do suffer immensely before finding a way to shift their thinking into a more positive process that allows them to again find some joy in their life. Many do much better than that.

I would also venture to say that you are one of those lucky ones that will do better than most. I know this because you are searching. You would not have picked up this booklet to read if you did not have that spark that is necessary to not only get out of the deep well you are in, but prosper through the process and end up much better than you had started. There is a wonderful quote by Joseph Campbell you may have heard, "It is by going down into the abyss that we recover the treasures of life. Where you stumble, there lies your treasure."

So why do we sometimes think life sucks? I believe it is because some, or even a lot, of the time life is horribly painful. And most often that pain comes from events and experiences that seem entirely out of our control. In fact, much suffering comes from simply not being able to enjoy what good we do find in life. This inability to see and enjoy good when often it is staring us in the face seems to clearly lie within ourselves; it feels as if it is some deep seated defect in our character. We can experience this sort of inner darkness through an acute depression that is not based on anything bad happening externally—a depression that just seems to linger for no real reason one is conscious of. Maybe something external triggered it, a loss, lack of money, a relationship going sour—or maybe not. Whatever it might be, it often brings about a deep sense of helplessness, lethargy, and a feeling we have no control over our own feelings or the events that seems to affect them. This feeling of loss of control comes with anxiousness and feelings of anger as well.

The operative word here is "control." If we could control the flow of happiness in our lives, limit the flow of badness and suffering, we then of course would not think life sucks so much. But we can't, or so it seems. But is that entirely true? We will talk about this a bit more in later chapters.

Right now we want to only concern ourselves with why

life seems to suck. What is it for you? Are you experiencing a bad relationship? Either with a partner who seems incapable of bringing any joy, love, or connection and meaning into your life, or are you looking for someone to bring meaning and joy into your life that seems impossible to find? Are you in a bad job? A job that has no passion for you, that is also dead and seemingly incapable of bringing you any fulfillment and satisfaction? Are you experiencing financial difficulties? Is money just impossible for you to acquire? To hold onto? Or even to spend properly in a meaningful and responsible way? Are you dealing with difficult health issues? Or difficult health issues that have overwhelmed any of your loved ones? Are you depressed? Anxious? Always angry? Always sad? Always dissatisfied? Do you find no meaning in life? Are you just finished, tired of trying, and feel dead to the world? Is it something else I haven't mentioned? Yes, life does seem to suck sometimes, doesn't it?

Needless to say there are many things in the larger picture of life on this planet that can really make us dislike living our own individual lives—global violence, rampant evil and human meanness, world poverty, global deceit, world hunger and illness which brings about global suffering—the list can go on and on. But very few people suffer these particular things directly, or for very long if they do. In fact, the people who are directly affected have a direct way to process their trauma, and it is quite common to see great manifestations of human compassion, heroism, empathy, and productivity during acutely difficult times such as war, natural disaster, and other such examples of severe suffering.

Although it is possible these larger global events can have a lasting and deep negative impact on our isolated individual life, more commonly what makes us feel as if life sucks are highly personal events and experiences, such as family issues, personal and intimate losses, personal health issues, work issues, and other things that happen within our own microcosm of experience. We may think "the world is going to hell" but usually that sort of outlook leads to action or its opposite, complacency, rather than mental illness and personal emotional suffering. This isn't always the case, and it is difficult to tell if a global psyche that is ill and dysfunctional has a profound negative affect on an individual. That affect however, in most cases, is secondary to the affect of the immediate here and now in our personal lives.

So life itself doesn't really suck, it is our own personal interface with the events of our life that have an impact on how we feel about it as well as the triggers in life that touch deeper unconscious realms and cause them to leap into action seemingly with little reason. Research has shown that even the wealthiest individuals are often depressed with feelings of lack, and conversely, some of the poorest, and in the most compromised health situations, are the happiest. The events of life itself are not really the issue...it is how we relate to them that can create a feeling that life sucks.

WHY LIFE DOESN'T SUCK

There are only two ways to live your life. One is as though nothing is a miracle. The other is as though everything is a miracle.

~Albert Einstein

So that brings us to why life doesn't suck. That is pretty obvious, and most of us, even while believing nothing good comes to us, do believe there is stuff out there that could make life really grand for us. Money, loving relationships, good jobs, a basket of puppies... Whatever it might be, it is out there, and only if it would come our way. But is this really true? Sure, having all these things would indeed feel good when we got them, but would it last? Research has shown that if we are not properly set up internally to appreciate thoroughly and sincerely what does come our way we will not be able to really connect with our abundant life and appreciate it thoroughly.

Imagine if you lost the ability to taste, or better yet, could only taste sourness. No matter how much wonderful and ecstatic flavor was lavishly slathered on your tongue you would not be able to appreciate it, and if by chance something sour was mixed in with all the joy and wondrous taste sensations, the sour is all you would experience. The psyche is similar in the sense that if it is not tuned in to recognizing and appreciating all the ecstatic sensations of life it will not be able to fully appreciate them. Yes, the sour is in there as well, but we are typically built to be able to take a certain amount of that sour and deal with it. Sometimes we can't, but it usually isn't because that is all that life is made of, it is because that is the only sensation we are capable of distinguishing and really experiencing.

Just like we thought about all the reasons we may find life sucking, let's take a moment to think of all the things in our life that are sweet tasting. Can you pick them out and at least see them? You may not be able to taste them yet, but can you recognize that they are there? Can you step around the shadow and see them? Granted, you may be dealing with a very big shadow right now, and maybe your feeling that life sucks is entirely circumstantial (such as the death of a loved one, or the loss of a good job). Typically you will be able to move through these life traumas without much outside intervention, although that isn't always the case and you may need a few helping hands along the way. For those of you that do wonder why life seems to continually suck, without any acute tragedy related to your feelings— or an acute tragedy that took place a long time ago such as child abuse—you may be able to at least *see* more clearly the sweets you should be tasting a bit more of.

Yes, life does suck sometimes. But as a whole it is important that it not suck, or at least we not perceive of it sucking all of the time, or sucking in general. It would be quite difficult to live a happy, meaningful, and fulfilling life with this perspective being the primary way you see life. Yes, right now you may feel this way, but let's try to see if there is anything you can do to change that view enough that you can begin to function in a more fulfilling way.

WHAT YOU CAN DO

"I can't do it," never yet accomplished anything; "I will try," has accomplished wonders; and "I am doing it" has created miracles.

~George P. Burnham

There are lots of things you can do, believe it or not. I don't want you to feel this is a simplistic approach to your not-so-simple problem. It isn't. But this is a little booklet aimed at maybe shedding some light on a more serious matter. Although it is true that thinking more positively, counting your blessings, and all the similar things you read about in self-help books will undoubtedly bring a better perspective into your awareness, I am not going to tell you that is what you need to do right now all at once. Maybe I will say eventually you will get to that point, but for the time being we will not go in that direction with too much fervor.

What you do need to do is start to break the cycle. This, I believe, you have already started by picking up and reading this book. This is a very important step, and holds more weight in your recovery than most anything else. You have to be ready for change, you have to admit that you want to change something, and you have to take the first steps in making those changes. You have already started, so congratulations!

Since everyone's issues are as unique as they are, it is impossible to give any specific instructions in this little booklet. As we have discussed various things about life and about suffering and where that suffering may come from and what it may look like we have only scratched the surface. Most of the negative action (the action of seeing the world as sucking and the action of responding to that in various ways—depression, anxiety, anger, etc.) comes from a place we are not even consciously aware of—the unconscious.

Although most conventional approaches in psychotherapy don't address the unconscious directly but instead look at very conscious ways to deal with the symptoms of mental illness and dysfunction, my belief is that the true problem, or at least the mechanism that creates the problem, lies in the unconscious. Little, or quite big depending on the issue, operating systems are created for various reasons through a person's life and are tucked away in the dark layers of the unconscious mind, actually living lives of their own that have no connection with the conscious thinking mind we navigate through our days with...with one major exception.

These independent systems can be triggered into action by information they receive through the conscious senses—a tone of voice from your partner, a boss's strange look, a general malaise every morning upon rising—bang...you are angry, depressed, fearful, anxious. You may even take intensive action or actions as you are being propelled by the desires and wishes of some powerful system you are otherwise wholly unaware of buried deep in the subconscious. These unconscious systems can be activated by major events as well, making them seem much bigger than they actually are.

Sounds like I'm making this up, eh? Hardly. This concept is pretty hard science and was pioneered by such great psychiatrists as Sigmund Freud, Carl Jung, and Alfred Adler, among many others. It's real, Trust me.

And there is definitely something you can do about it.

Why Life Sucks

Clearly I will say if your situation is debilitating for you, i.e., if you are having a difficult time functioning, if you are suicidal, or if the condition has lasted more than a few months or so, you should really seek professional help. Therapy is simply not a big deal if you are thinking it is. It is actually quite cool, and can help you in a lot of profound ways. So you should consider it. There is nothing more effective than journeying through the depths of the unconscious with a reputable and experienced guide.

In the mean time, start a journal. This is one of the most effective ways to tell the psyche that you are interested in doing something about the dissonance you are experiencing between your unconscious world and your conscious world. In addition to this, or in place of it, do a specific dream journal. Believe it or not, dreams are symbolic representations of what is actually going on in that unconscious mind of yours. It is like at night all those little demons and goblins come out and play and you get to watch them through a tiny window as you sleep. By the way, not all unconscious content is bad, far from it. There are wonderful delights to find there as well. It is typically the shadow content we repress, banishing it all to the dark recesses of the dungeon hoping to never see it again. There is little likelihood of all that dark stuff staying quiet, as it is quite angry with you for considering it bad in the first place. You see, in fact, none of it in itself is bad; it only can cause bad experiences in your life because it is unconscious and the unconscious bubbling up in unexpected ways can wreak havoc on your sense of control and rational mind.

So a dream journal is a good idea, as it takes all that material that is yearning to be known and brings it into a conscious realm—through you writing it down. It doesn't do to just think about it, you must write it down, preferably by hand, or you must tell it to another person, preferably a person who is unbiased, and even possibly a professional trained in working with dreams.

I would be remiss if I did not also give some time to the physical causes of depression and anxiety. Are you getting enough sleep? Are you exercising regularly? Are you eating a healthy diet? These things are more important than you may think, and they really should be the first line of attack if you are battling depression. I would also suggest a renewed relationship with nature—get out more often, at least once a day. Feel dirt between your toes and fingers, take a walk in the woods, stare into the mystery of an animal's eyes. These things truly have great power.

These are a few things you can start with. And if they don't clear up your issues in and of themselves, you may consider professional psychotherapy with a reputable and educated psychotherapist. That being said, undoubtedly it would be best to work with a professional from the beginning. Be careful in choosing one that you feel the fit is good and has experience in dream work and the unconscious.

WHAT YOU CAN'T DO

God grant me the serenity
to accept the things I cannot change;
courage to change the things I can;
and wisdom to know the difference.
~Reinhold Niebuhr

This will be a short chapter as these concepts are rather obvious, although ignored by most people. First of all, you can't depend on changing other people. I would be inclined to simply say you can't change other people, but that isn't altogether true. Obviously if you are with a partner that exhibits a behavior that you find very annoying you can always ask them to stop the behavior and often they do oblige, and thus change their behavior. The important point I am trying to make here is that you can't *depend* on someone changing in order to make your life happier, to make your troubles go away, or simply to function in a more meaningful and fulfilling way. This is quite important.

For just one isolated example: You can't make someone love you just so you can feel lovable and then dissolve into jelly if you are not successful. You can, however, attempt to make someone see something lovable about you through your actions, your demeanor, and your own unique personality. But if they pass, you should be able to pass as well (albeit with *normal* pain). Getting someone to love you doesn't define you; it can be a desire, but not a necessity. If it *is* a necessity, this is generally due to something hidden in your unconscious that says you can't live without it.

There are also quite a few other things you can't change, and you know what they are, we all know what they are, but we keep trying to change them. What we typically *can* change are things within ourselves, such as our behavior, our perspective, our compassion, our empathic nature, and our expectations. But there are even some things about ourselves that we can't change directly. If we have a major physical disability we typically cannot change that, only our attitude toward it. There are some forms of mental illness we cannot change within ourselves, but if you were suffering from one of these you probably would not be reading this booklet.

So then it erroneously seems that anything that matters we cannot change because all the things that seem to matter, and that make life not suck, are outside of ourselves and impervious to our effort to change them. Again, most things we *can* actually change, the key word here though is that we cannot *depend* on those things changing in order to be ok. This seems like a catch, and in a certain way it is a catch, and very difficult to get our head around. That is why so many people suffer through life. If it were that obvious I think we would just always do what is best for ourselves and be fine.

There is also that pesky unconscious to deal with, because even if we figure out this secret of the unconscious and its hidden control over us, we still have that whole battalion of nasty unconscious complexes trying to mess things up to get the attention they feel they sorely need.

So lets approach this from two fronts. The first front is taking control of what we can control—ourselves, our attitudes, and our attentiveness to life, pleasure, joy and beauty. We do this simply by finding the good in whatever we encounter no matter how elusive it may seem. Yes, at times we will not be capable of finding good in something, in those cases, leave it alone for another time. But in most things in our experience we can find joy if we look. Keep in your journal a "Gratitude Section" where you list all the things you are grateful for every day. They can be simple, and believe me; most of them are quite simple. That's the conscious front.

To deal with the unconscious turmoil taking place every day, keep your journal, and especially your dream journal. It would help too to find a creative activity if you don't already have one. The unconscious is accessed most readily through creative endeavor. Give it a try.

WHAT NOW?

Try the suggestions in this little booklet and see what happens. Depending on your situation you may see results right away. Most importantly, to begin with, you are paying attention to a wounded entity, your whole Self, not just the self you think is the whole you (the conscious ego self) but the Self that includes everything about you, the dark shadowy stuff as well as what you are consciously aware of. The attention alone is healing, as this whole part of you wants to be recognized and accepted and loved.

If things continue to get worse, please seek out professional help. I would recommend looking for a good psychotherapist who is well trained and well educated in this particular type of work. Needless to say this is what I specialize in. Take some time to visit my website at www.toddhayentherapy.com to learn more about my work, or choose one of my colleagues I have listed there if you prefer a female therapist or one in another area. You can also Google search your area for a good therapist.

Why Life Sucks

I hope this little booklet has at least opened the door for you with regard to your deeper discovery of the wonders of life. Needless to say life is a great gift and does not, in general, suck, far from it—although at times it certainly seems like it does. As I said at the beginning of this booklet, you are not alone, and there is help waiting for you. Now that you have taken the first step, take the next one, and follow yourself into a healthy, meaningful, joyous, and fulfilling life.

ABOUT THE AUTHOR

Todd Hayen, PhD, RP practices psychotherapy in Aurora, Ontario, Canada with his wife, Cindy Hayen, PhD, RP. They both use a variety of methodologies to facilitate treatment including depth psychology, psychodynamic psychology, transformative and transpersonal psychology and cognitive behavioral psychology. Visit their websites at:

www.toddhayentherapy.com and www.cindyhayen.com.